WAITING FOR MY CLOTHES

Leanne O'Sullivan was born in Cork in 1983, and is currently studying English at University College Cork. She has been writing poetry since she was 12, and has won most of Ireland's main poetry competitions, including the Seacat, Davoren Hanna and RTE Rattlebag Poetry Slam. Her poems have appeared anthologies including *Poetry 180*, edited by Billy Collins (Random House, USA, 2003), *The Backyards of Heaven: contemporary poetry from Ireland, Newfoundland & Labrador*, edited by Stephanie KcKenzie & John Ennis (WIT/Scop, Waterford & Newfoundland, 2003) and *The New Irish Poets*, edited by Selina Guinness (Bloodaxe Books, 2004), as well as in many Irish poetry magazines, including *Cork Literary Review*, *Poetry Ireland Review*, *The Shop* and *The Stinging Fly*. She has given readings in many places, from Ireland to New Mexico, and her poems have been broadcast on RTE radio.

LEANNE O'SULLIVAN

Waiting for My Clothes

BLOODAXE BOOKS

ISBN: 1 85224 674 X

First published 2004 by
Bloodaxe Books Ltd,
Highgreen,
Tarset,
Northumberland NE48 1RP.

Second impression 2005.

www.bloodaxebooks.com
For further information about Bloodaxe titles
please visit our website or write to
the above address for a catalogue.

Bloodaxe Books Ltd acknowledges
the financial assistance of
Arts Council England, North East.

Cover printing by J. Thomson Colour Printers Ltd, Glasgow.

Printed in Great Britain by
Cromwell Press Ltd, Trowbridge, Wiltshire.

For my family

ACKNOWLEDGEMENTS

Acknowledgements are due to the editors of the following publications where some of these poems first appeared: *The Backyards of Heaven: contemporary poetry from Ireland, Newfoundland & Labrador,* ed. Stephanie KcKenzie & John Ennis (WIT/Scop, Waterford & Newfoundland, 2003), *Cork Literary Review, Electric Acorn, The Dubliner, The New Irish Poets,* ed. Selina Guinness (Bloodaxe Books, 2004), *Poetry Ireland Newsletter, Poetry Ireland Review, Poetry 180: A Turning Back to Poetry,* ed. Billy Collins (Random House, USA, 2003), *The Shop, The Stinging Fly* and *Wildeside Literary Magazine.*

'Crescendo' won the Seacat National Poetry Competition in 2001, 'The Cord' won the RTE Rattlebag Poetry Slam and 'The Prayer' won the Daovren Hanna Award for Young Emerging Irish Poet, both in 2003.

I would like to thank Sue Booth Forbes for her huge encouragement.

CONTENTS

Poetry

I can never find a pen when you come,
when you snap me up on your lizard tongue,
and wrap yourself around me as if I were a spool.
Vague as metaphors you tease, trawling
your shadows as feathering clouds do,
shedding infant vowels in your vaporous image.
You will never be perfected,
and while you are half-born I will never sleep.

In pickling ink I preserve all your fruits;
perhaps you are a prophecy,
a mouthing of the boundless,
or some God or other Minerva festering
like secrets in empty lines.
Years gone now, labouring to drain
the reddest blood from your throat,
and I am none the wiser.

Earliest Memory

My memory is of her mouth moving
my name, syllable by restless syllable,
as my feet drum the foot-rest of the high-chair.

The apple-rind lies beside her elbow, curled
like cigarette smoke as she leans
forward on her stool, and the core,

scooped out, rests carefully in
the yoghurt-streaked carton, its pores
stand there gleaming and wide-eyed.

We are snapping sounds from the air –
the honeyed 'L', the pure mineral of the 'E',
the drone of 'Annnnnnnnnne'.

She throws my name upwards, her
throat like the neck of a lily,
she clears it and announces 'Naaaa-Na'.

I see myself in the well of her pupil
and rock desperately in the chair until
she piles the spoon full of yoghurt,

cleans the bottom and sides
with her peony lips, then
it chugs towards me. I lap it up,

balancing the spoon between my lips,
and again she folds the fruit and yoghurt
onto my spoon, lick by lick, mothering it

as if draining an egg of its white,
pouring from shell to shell, leaving me
with the pure gold, soft and tender as a breast.

Fishes

My friend moves her pink crayon in the tough
awkward way she rocks her doll to sleep,
as if trying to get the best out of that stick
of wax, every last paring. She disguises
the fish with luminous pink, a wax that
cannot be eaten, cannot be burned.

Her paper bulges like an angry blister.
It was a fine fish, with a sliver of moonlight
in its pupil, its thick black membrane, slightly
broken at the fin. I polish the outline
of my drawing with my finger.
Fish are silver, I say.
Her pink crayon slows like the brake
of a locomotive. She lifts her cheek
from her hot palm, looks at me
and says, I'm seven. And fishes are pink.

We eat some chocolate, and I give her
chewing gum. After she's gone outside
I take the pink wax, lean tremendously
on my elbow and onto the wax,
melting the rule and watching
with my mouth slightly open as
the pink and silver fish roars.

Perfect Disorder

There is a disease spreading across this island.
The fields are already dark and vacant,
foodstuffs lie rotting by the gates.
I come with my brittle candle and faded map.

I have no cure but need. When every omen
is thrusting towards the end of a life,
when, on the calmest day, an empty look steals
the most radiant smile, I have no cure.

Eagerly, a shop assistant tells a ten year old
her jeans are slimming. The mothers say *eat*.
The mothers ask what is wrong. The doctors
say *eat*. The doctors say there is nothing wrong.

But the shame of this infection – when we cast
our eyes hellwards, re-inventing beauty
with deranged applause as another pound is lost,
puts its burning face in our hands.

Perhaps this battle will end like others –
wresting mothers from daughters, fathers
from mothers, flesh from blood,
killing us along with the killers,

and leaving the safest roads overgrown.
The disease infects a thought or a void,
creates hatred in innocent blood.
The young and old are dying together.

It is not a myth, or a story in black and white.
It is my face in your daughter, my vacant stare
in your husband's eyes, my hand in your hand,
squeezing it very tightly, saying, *Don't look away.*

When We Were Good

The girl and I face each other.
She is twelve years ago,
her little body framed in long,
looping curls, her torso bent
under the load of her schoolbag.
I see her goodness,
her ruddy face flushed, beaming.
I want to tell her
bad things will happen;
fingertips will rove spirals around
her chest, starting at her tummy,
kneading her pleated breast
like a cold stethoscope,
and she will conceive
it before it happens,
will allow flesh to web
all the silky threads of her,
and she will close
her eyes while it happens,
going back to novels, mermaids –
back to Nana,
to biscuits in bed –
back to the beginning
of the world
when everything was small
and so far away;
and she was all goodness,
looking up at the world
blindly, like a girl under a boy.

Famine

The girl sits at the dinner table
during the throb of winter,
the famine of the 90s, sullen,
eyes narrowing at the place of rice,
lips parting and slamming in the draught
as the raw cold wind bellows outside.

Starvation and adolescence are piercing
her in turns. She pushes herself back
on the rosewood chair, layers of clothes
hugging her in the kitchen heat,
the new boundaries of her chest aching.

She is beautiful,
but each day she bruises her spine on
rosewood, pinches the flesh on her thighs,
her peninsular hips.
She believes her stomach is swelling
with the heat like bread.

She says to her mother, as the plate
inches away, *I ate earlier*,
and she folds her arms over the guilt
that is filling her.

Slowly, along her spine
soft, quilted hairs grow,
for her life, devoted as prayers.

Sliocha Nan Ron

(Children of the Seals)

When I remember my sixteenth year
I hear my grandmother telling me of selkies,
seals that took the form of women on land,
letting fall their smooth skin on the shore,
bathing and dancing in moonlight with their new bodies.

After she told me I went to the beach near our house,
I ran to it as if I would never let the dawn take
my smooth, child's skin from me. On the driftwood
dead starfish lay like garlands of fruit, flowered,
and orphaned from the starless night.

Nothing was clear. The moon peeled the ocean back
and I saw a woman in a pane of water, a hip first, a breast.
What happened between the sand and the ocean
happened in darkness, slowly fingering the base aside,
each jewel disappearing easy as a breath.

The ocean was birthing this new creature to land,
it folded and gathered like a sheet as I entered the soft
pelt of the waves. The ocean had been sailed,
the horizon tender for my outstretched limbs,
my open mouth, my tapered legs moving into deepness.

I moved towards the large waves.
I moved to preserve this child in cold salt.
And as the starfish let go of the driftwood,
as the wind blew the springs back towards the mountain,
the sun began to rise, and the water washed over my head.

Mirror

The image grew there,
just as a child would grow,
a private hope in that tunnel skin
of my mind. I saw I existed.
I saw two where there should
have only been one.
Divided, the image
climbed into my head
and that foetus flooded
my guilt, until nothing explained
my life better than these
clothes falling to the floor.

I was caught in her eye,
caught red-handed.
I called her the skinny saint.
I called her the beautiful bitch.
Then she took my real eyes
and tongue and made them hers.
I could barely name myself.
I wear black, because black
is what she wants to see –
a hole, a cover, a hatred that
goes in search of something hateful,
going in search of a mirror.
And I stare, and scorn,
and pinch, spitting through tears,
Woman, I know you not.

My Father's Fleece

At school the radiators are on the ceiling
and the heat is fed to an icy sun,
its white flames lapping up the drizzle.

I wear my father's fleece like folds
of drapery; Ireland green,
I wear it all day when a pulse flakes

from summer, and in class I curl
my flesh into my bones, pull
my arms from the sleeves

and couch into it, green and small
as the seedling I was in the womb.
Smelling his aftershave on the collar

I can take a kiss from his leather cheek
after one Sunday night cigarette.
When I try to quit smoking

I swaddle my chin and chew at the zipper,
as a babe does her mother's fingers.
In that pure cavern I am child of my father –

breasts shallow, hips a levée;
a sacred topography. I sleep in my fleece
during any ice, curl my flesh

into my bones, pull my arms from the sleeves
and draw my legs into the green core,
only my hair visible.

Bulimic

Blood dries on the bathroom floor
beside my head as I lie curled in
a foetal ball watching dripping pipes.

I am a dirty puddle of darkness after purging.
In black clothes on a bed of polar tiles
my back yawns bare between a belted waist

and little top, silently awing the still tub.
The dim moon of my body is shocked
by pale shores of arms and neck and face,

made paler still by moonlight and stars.
At midnight the bathroom is hushed.
Ingrained in the circle of my dead gaze

the toilet stops hissing. Innocent
as a lunatic I knelt hours ago before it,
hearing a skinny saint rave within me –

'Empty, empty her and she'll be thin!'
I clung to the covenant like clingfilm
over a rib and heaved her hungers.

Drunk on her breath and bowed
to a cistern I emptied, emptied,
emptied her,

burned her weeds and wiles –
I trespassed into the body's chambers
and raped it with two blistering fingers.

This fire may lick and melt
but it is unforgiving; my fingers
may enter but parch and scorch

in the caustic passion of juices from the gut.
The body weeps, reluctant.
Be wary of it.

She erupts maniacally
until blood makes her holy, barren, empty.
Neither tears nor the easy flush

can patch a ceremony. It escapes
into the eve of thinness.
The cold body keels in honeyed drips

onto tiles; knees collapse,
elbows dance graceless
from the seat; a demented head

falls on a scale, blood trickling from the nose.
Now, curled beside dripping pipes,
weighing the head's load, in black clothes

framing the arms, the neck, the face.
The tiles do not warm the numb.
We move like spirits.

The Cord

I used to lie on the floor for hours after
school with the phone cradled between
my shoulder and my ear, a plate of cold
rice to my left, my schoolbooks to my right.

Twirling the cord between my fingers
I spoke to friends who recognised
the language of our realm. Throats and lungs
swollen, we talked into the heart of the night,

toying with the idea of hair dye and suicide,
about the boys who didn't love us, who
we loved too much, the pang of the nights.
Each sentence was new territory, a door

someone was rushing into, the glass shattering
with delirium, with knowledge and fear.
My mother never complained about the phone bill,
what it cost for her daughter to disappear

behind a door, watching the cord
stretching its muscle away from her.
Perhaps she thought it was the only way
she could reach me, sending me away

to speak in the underworld. As long as
I was speaking she could put my ear
to the tenuous earth, allow me to listen,
to decipher. And these were the elements

of my mother – the earthed wire,
the burning cable – as if she flowed
into the room with me to somehow say:
Stay where I can reach you, the dim room,

the dark earths. Speak of this
and when you feel removed from it
I will pull the cord and take you
back towards me.

The Quest

When I found my grandmother
in the middle of the night, she was half
out of bed, one leg angling over the side,
her arms reaching out to me, like
the carving of Jesus Christ on her nightstand.

Physical, penetrating, breathless,
she swore that she saw something move
in the hallway, stammering across
the ribbon of light under the door.
I imagine her watching the yellow

sliver for a sign of life to travel
the length of it, waiting to be drawn to it,
as if she had glimpsed something worth taking;
light, shadow, light like heaven
in the darkness of her bedroom.

I took her open hands and helped
her up. I could hardly move her,
the whole century of her leaned on me,
gripped me with fingers so kneaded
together like a cable, eyes narrowing –

little heaven fires as she drew herself
forward, her weight heaving on the floorboards.
She went toward it with the same burst
she had left the womb. A lambency lit
in her eyes, I could see the filament

growing as we stepped along the beam
of light, her mouth open, wordless
as the flood came upon her face, a child
entering into the world, the tympanic
beat of her heart, breath rasp and shallow,

inching into the brightness with fervour.
And like a God, Grandmother,
I deliver you to it.

My Father Asks Me Why

How could he have known?
The nights I forced myself
to stay awake doing sit-ups,
up and down, up and down...

And when I nearly passed out
the skinny saint chanted
and numbers lay across the plate
of my mind. She never let me
rest, and my parents being
somehow bound to me
never slept. At first light,
when the world hatched,
I unrolled my body from cramps,
and ran in light clothes,
knowing that my body
ate itself in the cold,
pared itself down, like a sculpture,
to something that was always
'nearly perfect'.

My father couldn't have known
that all the while I still
believed I was going to win,
bone, blood, and chill.

Father, I only think to number
another mile, going round and round
the neighbourhood, like a rumour.

The world burns out, and flips over,
turns inside out, the cold side
of a hospital pillow, a dead life.

The Suicide

She didn't know an overdose wouldn't kill for days
till she was perched beside her daughter's poisoned
body, in the intensive care unit.

The girl's head propped on a pillow, her pale, hollow-bellied
form sucking on the paps of oxygen.
Mother is pregnant again.

Daughter conceived that June morning by love
as the girl's naked chest rose
and fell, in and out, back to then and out again.

Birth stain of charcoal around the petals
of her lips, her hair dew drizzled, a body
clammy and gleaming.

A lifeline rose on her upturned palms.
The monitors pressing her to the earth,
hauled by will to their green summits by a mother

who choked and contracted, hunch-backed,
signing papers. By heart she holds here Barbie dolls,
basketballs, awards, her husband's child.

She can't remember anymore the moment
she bent to take them, turning on her heel
and packing them away.

She remembers the pulse of bearing her,
as the baby muddled along the passage,
eyes narrowing, and limbs shouldering

aside the soft walls, she emerged writhing,
snatching breath,
nuzzling into the breast of her father.

The Ward

Waking in winter, pulling the curtains
from around my bed I smell

the tin of the food, the sultry weather
of the TV room, leather chairs

reeking in terrible heat.
Sunlight flays a glass

of cranberry juice – and each
anaemic patient collapses

into her Ophelia, touching
flowers on her bedspread.

Medicine Man

Medicine Man,
the room is a little wobbly,
your face is leaning like Pisa,
you are giving me so much!

Three on my tongue every evening,
like keys for some lock
and my mouth is the door swinging.
I close it and burn.

The radio plays some beat,
and it is crashing into my room,
like a hundred moths.
Over my body the drums go.

The music moves more
than I do. Medicine Man,
you're a crazy man.
I've been doped.

This morning I was numb,
now my body opens and stretches like a cut.
What a party this is! You turn
off the light, but it turns into fire,

a spotlight for my dance.
My mind is swinging. I hear it
like a chorus of bells, my limbs
thrust wildly as if pushing a

boulder away from a tomb.
Man, here is your experiment.
Heaven and hell are drowning
in the fire of dance.

I wrap myself in a dirty sheet and have not
a strap of fear until you tie me down.
Medicine Man,
the dancer has gone out.

A Thing of Beauty

They see from the supermarket aisles,
from school hallways and kitchen windows,
she is moving, all bone and teeth, hips winking,
ribs smiling; her eyes are curtains stirring
blindly in the dark, moving in circles.

Sweet emptiness, women glide towards her
as if on air, loving bone better than hunger.
How did you lose it? Your hands exquisite as sapphire,
the heart drumming like a tap-dancer's shoes –
you look so well! And thinner still, a daughter,

a sister, a scholar; she is not there.
There are words that rot here. Beauty,
or some other venerable word lies on their tongues
like a cherub. Women in short dresses and suits
holding their books and babies, drop their loads to adore.

Many women sing; beauty as soft as downy hair,
beauty bright as bone, eyes dead as marbles.
Mouths are opening, saying nothing.
They are women, mothers, nuns,
bloated by their hungers, fattened by some guilt.

We become sculptors. Beauty is the shape of love.
A skeleton as prone to worship as a Goddess
is by many called beautiful, or worse,
a hunger that teaches power.
We look; she's gone. Brutally perfect.

The blood crawls from her face. She collapses
and the whole world gathers around in decay.
She's dying, beauty's undoing. We say to her
yes, yes, you're a beautiful corpse,
Congratulate, congratulate.

Rite of Passage

I love to hurl my body into the ocean,
gliding over the pier. As if a God
had let me fall I am caught
then saved by that deep, pure well
of another life, the low hum of it around me,
seeping inside me like a sperm to an egg.

On the shore I can only see the swell,
the tide that opens and swallows
like a great beak. I swim hard,
as if something's being conceived
and I am at the centre of it,
not yet breathing, but alive.

Sometimes I am afraid to open my eyes
to the salt, and the cadence like muscle
against my body as I pull myself forward.
I feel the ocean itself is flesh,
and the delicate psalm of the heart is
beating somewhere in the core,

as if all the earth were a cell
and I am the life in the elements,
breaking out to the surface
at the bottom, my fingers
clawing the base of a miracle,
the cut-throats spawning.

Being Free

Once I did, I escaped
through a crack in the window,
that precious gash which broke
the monotony of our reflections
and the TV's binding hue.

It was late that night, when quite
suddenly I felt that I was free.
I flowed outside with the heat,
my eyes wandered down
the hospital route, following
the silhouettes, down and down
until I could taste the sea,
opening my mouth like a flower
and throwing my head back
as if I were on the edge of a pier.

I was surrounded by heaven,
counting the stars,
and they followed me,
like eyes in a photograph,
as I floated along the rocks
and touched upon the shore,
and sang my heart to the sky,
and drowned my hate in the sea,
and my strength marched along
the sky, taking me into him
until I was fulfilled,
looking upon it all with peace.

Once I did, I escaped,
through that crack in the window,
with the heat.

The Fruit

During the long, idle nights of summer rain,
I sit at my desk conceiving poems,
spilling them like birth milk onto the page.
There's a half bottle of stale orange-juice
standing like a soldier in vigil on my desk,
it has been there for so long that I cannot
remember when I needed it.
When I think it is time to throw it out
I notice the hissing, then the colonies
of fungus, globes against the sun,
the bubbles rising to the surface like
a flower towards light, and the pulp
swimming like eggs in the warm core.
The foam breathing steadily, I sit at my desk,
in dumb human earnest, watching
the relic fluid, the old juice conceived
out of fruit, the fruit, unwanted, thriving.

By Night

So many walls,
so many doors,
though only one exit;
yet friendship prospers
as dusk descends.
Whispers surpass walls,
prayers, a rosary
trickles from this
corner and that room.
We cede the moon to its purpose
and dream.

A Prayer I Said That Winter

Running her fingers through
her rosary beads, a nun told
the patients that God moves
in mysterious ways.

God moved maniacally
within us, behind pillars
and doors and crosses
that justified his will.

God grew beside me,
a great tree, its branches rising
as if it were reaching towards
something heavenly.

All autumn the tree
shed its leaves and stood
in vigil outside the ward, its purpose
hidden. I'd pass it on my way

to the Chapel, and somewhere
inside me I knew that believing
is seeing, that the force of earth
would nourish my dead soldier,

take his limb and haul him
towards me. I remember little
of that winter, until it came
to be spring. As I watched,

the tree exalted in the warm, liquid air,
full-leafed and dazzling, reaching out
like a prophet, its hands
full of fruit, witness of this earth.

Hunger

If I could kill
one thing
in my body
I would murder this:
a furious hunger that
is in me, that runs through me like the beat
of a song whose name I can't remember,
until the hunger becomes its own torch
in the night.
And I drown in it,
fall into
a silent age,
listening to words
fly past my ears like wind – and it is day,
then dusk, then day again.
I forget I have a name or have
even been born.
Looking
down
at my nose,
left to right, getting lost
in the thought that I may not even be,
the sun and the moon passing
in front of my eyes like schizophrenic visions.
I do not
hear my body
leave me,
my mind, my lips.
I look through my eyes
as if through a kaleidoscope,
watching my arms gathering
all my lovers into them,
hauling them over the border
where it is gagged and cold,
and the ice,
like fire,
burns
the driest flame.

These are the kisses
remaining on my mouth like a scar.
And if I could make peace
with it – if I could give
anything of mine
so that I could
be tamed
then I
would
give this.

For My Brother

We are here again, my room at 2 a.m.
after a gig in the pub; you, lying on the floor,
palms empty without your guitar,
me on my bed, pouring cigarettes
into my body. You say they'll kill me,
I say, I'm never leaving this earth.

We are Gods already, immortal and pissed,
taking on life. We talk about life a lot,
mostly on these Friday nights when you are
drunk on the music and the applause, and I
am drunk with pride, when it all seems good.

Our eyes pinned to each other we talk,
the night curved over us like a womb.
This is the safe time, when the world is
asleep and we can bitch about it.
Tonight you tell me that you love
talking to me. This is the life

of the Gods; brother and sister twinned
as if inside our mother, before light
opened her and we twisted, separate,
before we could decipher what was mine
and what was yours. Once again we have

a new flesh, a strange light making us,
and once again you are the first thing I see.
Sometimes we cry over our adolescence,
and we move closer as if we are
trying to escape it by being nearer.

I look at your silky eyes, seeing myself
in you, seeing you in myself, the same blood.
You top my cigarette, holding me
and saying, These will kill you.
I give to you, you take from me,
you hold me, but I steady you.

Hangover of Years

In the bathroom I hit the floor,
sweating and freezing, my heart

stammering and stopping the way
my tongue did when I needed a lie.

I'd spin all those white words like webs.
The truth never twitched like this.

My body fed on pain, the breast of dawn
and holy nights of punishment.

As I shackled myself
to these muses I used to smile.

I never felt my good heart cry.
She had stayed so quiet. I thought

I was spoiling her with my act of shrinking,
as if she would grow instead of me.

She is waking up today,
this limb in my chest is shaking

and shaking the cradle of my body,
like a mother gone mad from pain.

What Doesn't Kill Us

They'd bring a tray to my room
and place it on a table, then leave me there
facing that bowl of lumpy soup,
one slice of bread, leaving me there
to live and kill. The bitch burned
in me, squalling my head
with her denials. I could have killed
the two of us, but we fed
on each other, like plants and animals,
the breath we inspire.

It hurt to smother her, but the pain
was not shrill. The bread was soft,
I held it to my mouth like a bandage
and cried into it. It was the perfect crime,
the scoop, the curve, the kill and return.
I sat in front of that bowl like it was
a mound of leeches that drank
the pulse of her, spoonful
by spoonful, so I would not die.

Wild and starved I drained it
until I could stand above her
and I heard her fall, the old black heart
growing thin and dead as meat.
I would murder, or she would thrive
on any terms including my life.

Earth

At the height of the day, the fragile wing
of a cloud. It seems like nothing could
survive here, the dirt on the ground slightly
puckered in the thick heat.
I hear a cricket's sleek music moving
up from the ground, and imagine
its head flung back in awe of quiet.
Then the sound opens in another place,
a fall of gems into the air
and onto the ground, moving away
from me or closer, my movements
silencing or inspiring the pulse.
The air is dry and hot.

Starting beneath the earth a willow
splits the ground and silently grows
towards its heaven, its branches and leaves
falling around me like a communion veil
above old blades of thorns.
And the grass smells like memories,
the small foliage folding and unfolding,
dark, slow, bouquet and leaf.
The willow knows, and it told me,
Always grow, stand as high as you are
and look around, protecting what is sacred.

Mourning

I stand before the water;
what satisfaction it has

in ebbing and flowing,
pining after lost land

yet giving and giving
to the storm ridge,

inheriting for its labours
an empty beer bottle,

rejected driftwood,
royalties of its endeavours.

We'll go to it anyway,
though it is the definition

of utter madness to
dwell on past indifference.

Some have oceans
of knowledge to feed

their tears, yet not a glass
to justify their joy.

This is no night to sink in,
no world to give in to.

I Live
(for Mary Madison)

I paced the hallway of the ward,
heaven to earth, trembling as if some master
had torn me like a flower, the soil opening
like a wound and shaken from the roots,
leaving me nameless and bare, my robe
hanging from my shoulders, the belt
like a half-hearted noose. They called
my name, a military conscription.
I walked in. He said,
'You will die without treatment.'

This is the moment, growing larger
by my life, growing older by the weed.
This hour, what is to die
will be sleepless, what is living
will blaze. The pine floor did not
quake, the walls did not crumble,
my file remained unopened.
I said nothing, only stood and ran.
If it was to be life, it would be passion.

The Prayer

Night after night I turn off the light
having done all I could have done,
yet my sister reaches above our bodies
to turn it on again. Then she toddles over
to the window to draw the curtains,
the lambency of the full moon
exhaling on her small face.
God bless Mommy and God Bless Daddy,
she whispers as she gets into bed with me,
her sleepy weight nuzzling into the womb
I have prepared for her. I look down
and see her staring at the moon,
her white hands clasped tightly,
palm to palm, holding her prayer up
to the burnt out sky, as if all her blessings
were held in that chamber, and she's delivering
their names to the care of some guardian;
God bless my family and all my friends
and my Nana in heaven
and my Granddad in heaven.

My God, I love this child, one knee
raised as if she is kneeling before
her listener, the steady throb
of prayer from her mouth, wrist,
palm, offering what she knows,
lying in utter abandon with the sheets
thrown off her, as if she's driving away
anything that might smother her,
her chest rising in righteousness, her hands
uplifted like one who hasn't given enough.

Claiming Lee

At dinner, I think of you walking
towards me, the nurse turning the key
in the door, like a penny in a fountain,
and your scent dances into my blood.
All your miracles throb in my throat.
You thought I hated you in
my hungry church. But never did
I want you so much as these last
few months of your mother hymns,
the nurse saying your name,
your breath through the phone,
the car on the gravel.

How I regret your pain when
what keeps me from dying is
the memory of falling asleep
with my face burrowed in your arms,
a prayer book in your hands.
Or today, in the moment between
wanting and thinking I have,
you wrap your arm around my waist
and kiss me. Your clear eyes brimming,
expecting me to say goodbye to you.

A Map of the World

I remember this woman who'd sit
for hours in the TV room, staring through
the window at the days and nights,
her winged arm hanging over the sill
as if she were in a car travelling
at a great speed. Once, after I was
forbidden to walk on the grass,
I sat beside her in a shaft of sunlight
as she told me how she had loved
the silk shawl of her garden back home,
walking barefoot there at night.
Then she took my hand in hers, the way
you would touch a flower, and slowly
traced each line of my life,
her fingers moving upwards like blood
from my vein, to the hollows of love
in my palm. I felt myself come alive
with her touch, as if continents were
pulling together inside me, the core fluid
with tremendous magma. My hand,
a landscape of earth; I walked it,
caressed the map which felt
like birth, death, heaven on earth,
the heat of hell, the blue stems
like labyrinths under a valley of flesh.
I was the ocean orbiting the shore,
a drowned man kissing the land,
surrounded by that strange smell of air.
How to move, I was not sure, my feet
spread on the ground like roots.
I leaned forward to kiss this woman's eye
and stood up, taking my first step towards
something that would survive me.

Hijacking Mom

I pictured you, Matthew, keeping vigil
by the ward doors, caught in a pillar of light
like the kneeling Mary Magdalene
by the garden of Gethsemane, fired
in sallow clay. How the ache must have
prickled and pushed you when the lock
clicked in the doors. Smooth as the pearl
of an oyster you slid through the thin
opening, your robe pouring and flapping
behind you, a circus awning. Bold
as a gull, an entourage of nurses trailing,
you dived into the heat of Mother's car.
'Drive!! Drive, fucking drive!!'
I imagine you, feeble as far off thunder,
hauled from our red Toyota, branded
with your sedative, tugged by the leash
of your robe back inside the hospital.
You'd guzzled your ration of air
and succumbed to the terrible dim
of valium, ativan, and other kisses
while your heart still beat to old poetry –
drive, fucking drive. I see you,
Matthew, bedraggled, kneeling
as Mary Magdalene, enlaced in
moonlight, counselled by Gethsemane.

Crescendo

Driving to my doctor in July, I sit
with my feet on the dashboard, calves
glinting in the white heat, a new lexicon
crawling around the corners of a napkin

as I try to write against my thighs. Above
our red Toyota the branches and leaves
of Ireland have kindled with the sky,
a Monet where there was once a Cézanne.

My mother seeks out the straightest routes,
allows the car to ebb the smooth middle
of the road as the wind laps the rim
of the window, staccato to the music

of Cat Stevens. I think she loves
the passion of overtaking, the thunder
of engines flirting on opposite sides
of the road. The corners of her eyes

will sharpen. Her stomach will tense
and flatten. Lips taut, she takes the reins
of our lives with both hands,
and as I close my eyes she delivers me

to the darkness just before birth, the pulse
of gears aroused, swelling, like the hum
induced by speed. We slide along the vein
of Mom's road, our bodies moving through

the air like seeds through a pistil, and when
I can feel my hair whipping my jaw again
I open my eyes and glance at my mother,
strands of her hair tucking in the salty tattoo

of the wind, her elbow angling over the lip
of the door. We descend, sending loose chips
flying like progress. She drives faster and faster
as if she's driving to save my life. We're falling

through the green of Ireland and Mom has
the gear-stick in her fist, as if it's the strong
branch of a tree to cling to. I change stations
on the radio, touching her fingers.

Getaway Car

At night, in the winter, we'd drive.
My father would ease into the driver's seat
and ignite the deep throat of the car,
his head tilted towards mine with love.
He would take me away from my mind,
into the dark with the headlights of his car
bulging out, as if we knew where we were going,
speeding over the black lining

of a bridge, until my thoughts couldn't
keep up with the road. Inching up
to the pier, the end of this world,
I felt fear leaving me, so close
to the edge, with my father's breath
pulling me back. We drove like this,
night after night, stopping here and there
where a gale let itself loose like
a kennel of dogs, or where a boy
stood flushed at a fork.

Side by side at the beach we sat away
from nothing, the black hole of it rising
above the sea, pressing against
the membrane of my father's car.
And my father let the radio play
till I didn't care about the blackness,
or the cold. I was warm, the headlights
licking the knees of an ocean,
the light of my father
at the end of a long black tunnel.

Honour

I ask for something to eat
and your heart leaps
into your throat,

Mother, standing by the grill
seasoning toast the colour
of your hair, your

face glows with the pride
of a praised child. You face
me with a slab of butter

that looks more like a doorstep.
I glance at the runny bread
and watch you watch me eat,

you sit so still,
the curve of your chin pointing
towards me as a woman

stretching her neck for musk.
I lap it slowly, that cryptic scent
of your perfume

and I take the bread we
took together at my christening,
at my first communion,

as if I could honour
your giving my life
by nourishing it with you.

What We Bear

It is December and she is barefoot.
She has packed her things, her jewels,
dirty laundry strewn on my bedroom floor
since I was born. I hear her closing
the bathroom door, switching off
the light, humming in one room or another,
her melody knelling through the house
like a banshee, declaring death.
She has picked the blood from the white walls,
grain by grain, as if it were mildewed paint.
My heart has long since stopped giving it;
she's become a corpse every time I look at her.
She'll perish without my eye, my lung,
her dead body folding in a box.
Each urn of water empty, she leaves me.
I see her head nod above the ditch,
like a dying flower in winter,
as she descends to a country
far away from thought.

The Fires That Move Through You

How far gone am I from the wound?
There is blood chilling in my limbs –
these legs were the bribe and I gave
my crutch, Adam's sickly rib.
These nights terrify me,
the ruined homesteads of dread
with doors swinging open like cradles.
It is the heartland that was charred.
It is one tongue out of the land
that was silenced. I will get back there,
for I have grown fond of remembering
all the moments between wars.

I am so slow, there is no patience
in the day, the sun wrapping up her coats
and turning in her black grave.
In the dark nothing is without a ghost
that haunts the steps left behind.
The red-head disappears like a priest
into the church. I am breathing like
the sea – many breaths, my hair rattles,
my legs drag me over the bridges.
I shall gag the dead, for I have
become old trying to forget.

How far am I from the scar?
It is one look of death that seduces war
and all that misfortune has reaped,
while life, who trembles on the shelf,
buries the threat that tried to bury her.
The soft, strange rumours of light
invite my lips like still waters.
My heart is weary from the passage,
but my legs have grown strong.
I am stepping out of Mars
and I am bringing water,
red as my cold, old face.

Comrades

(for Susan)

My heart's saviour,
my best friend, hear my voice
though distance overwhelms
and you waver between instinct and science.

Allow memory to rule over mind, over matter,
believe we can go beyond any distance,
believe I can clasp your hands
when they do not know where to reach.

Remember how our eyes bridged our souls.
Remember the bridge,
that linked the days we endured.

If These Walls Could Talk

If these walls could talk
they would drop, sheer as cascades
the silent conversations.
They stand erect like
the pricked ear of a fox,

darkening the grey pupil
of your eye to march across
the contours of my face.
The gilt moons of your fingertips
trace the curve of my cheek,

the stem of my throat,
the blue of my wrist.
You are my landscape,
the mountain, the sky,
your hair a shouldering spray.

You are my earth,
mountains folding in
from the core, eclipsing
the blue moons of my eyes.

The sun rolls back, slanting
to night, and we speak
in strange tongues,
our best syllables silent,
echoing like creviced caverns.

Your lips – two fires
to melt my cheek of wax.
Air silk, you fill
me like new secrets.
My mouth to your ear,
our skins make poetry,
ink rushing from our pores.

Positive Addiction

Do you hear it?
I wonder what you look like
when you're not draped in paper,
when your hands are washed of ink.

Sometimes you seem to be
making something, wrapping
yourself in trailing patchwork,
as if for someone to follow you by.

I wonder what you look like
under those rags, that woman
flesh lying like petticoats,
warm resin of birth.

I love the sound of you
pounding out your steps,
your shoes gathering dust
of days spent reddening
and browning, the way
rain meets nails.
                    Running,
as if a woman is a song
as if a body is a drum
as if a trail is a door
as if there is something
you could love more.

And you run to hearten
new flesh, the old given
to survival, the long road
like a razor, the edge
you do not wish to clutch.
Running, kicking back
old sand, as if it's your wish
to find something that would
hold you to this world.

Waking

In America, when the light rises and cups
the pearl of the mountain, like Eve slowly
raising her white face to the fruit tree,
I lie out on the veranda and watch the long skies
open like fingers from their dark palms.

Feeling beneath me the ripe land
that tumbles root-first into the gorge,
I throw a petal into the tremendous distance
and count the seconds of the fall.
It's no matter to be another drop of dust

in the pit where so many dead leaves
circle the earth in their old religions,
having nothing more to do with flesh or bone,
man or woman. The sun rises with complete knowing
of the day, folding the darkness into the gorge

with the aim of an eye. Meanwhile,
the people wake. A mother bathes her child,
the fisherman brings the sweet water to his mouth,
the gardener plucks the hopeless deadhead
from the stem, and so many things come to pass.

The Journey

We were on a train to Cork. She was seven.
It was cold and late. We had been on the train
for three hours. She was leafing through

my biology textbook as if all those inner regions
were works of fiction. She learned how to say
epiglottis and duodenum. Then she kneeled

on the seat to stare at her body in the black window,
her fingers tracing her frame, inhaling
so deeply to push that dome up and out,

and then pulling it in until she could grasp
the curved gate of her rib cage, as if she wanted
to open up her whole breast like a trapdoor to see

the base of her life. Then she looked at my face
so severely, *Where does the baby go?* she asked.
I said it grows behind your tummy, in your womb.

She took it in as if something had been thrust to her.
I could sense it slowly entering her,
and for a moment I saw it all, the promise of her,

the light fibres being spun behind her tummy,
her hips as small as two fists pressed together,
reaching back into that unripe nest,

dripping like a torch in the rain.
When she was satisfied, she curled up
on the seat the way she does when tired,

her arms like a blanket, protecting
what she did not know, the train
trembling on the outskirts of some city.

Autobiography

When I was a child I became a woman.
I was nine. It happened on a day
of drubbing sun while I was eating
a bowl of Cheerios. I leaned my trunk
across the table, the topography
of my chest painfully deeper, undulating.

I curled my chin into my neck and stared down
at the puffed drapes of my once pleated breasts.
I ran from the conservatory sun, thinking,
'Bollocks! The light's attracting them!'

Intoning the names of Jesus, Mary
and St Joseph, my mother stopped collecting
Cheerio coupons and bought a bra.
In the lingerie aisles I murmured confidentially,
touching like membranes the lace cups.

And now here I am; my contours
arched as the lip of a mug –
pink-bellied woman, squatting
in a darkened hallway, letting
a boy caress my cheek.

First Boyfriend

We avoided each other at all costs,
our paths crossing as if by accident.
He would pass me in the school halls
like a thought, the roar of the other students
dulling as we tried to burrow into it,
eager to pretend we were learning
something mindless. He would laugh
ridiculously at nothing, I would examine
my nails as if I could tear him
out of my vision like a hair.

We were building a school
and we were demolished by it,
standing beneath it on a Friday night,
beneath a street lamp on the corner
of some street, the amber light spilling
like honey with the drizzle.
We seemed to know each other well enough
to believe we had wished for this,
swelling like fuchsias and bursting open,
horrified by our impulses as if
they'd been bred by some other world
lost and then recovered.

I could have died, I could have lived
in this silence, moving towards this boy
as if he were forbidden. At school
I entered a new age with new blood
in my flesh, breathing,
                    'I could've died,
I could've died.' He sat away from me
in class, a feather of a dandelion
I had kissed. I looked as he looked away,
the cry of the teacher summoning us,
his strange face returning us to ourselves
as we turned the pages of our algebra formulas,
highlighting, considering, forgetting.

By Ear

There was always a piano, a sound
not like the thunder of rock or metal,
but soft, like the wind of a hymn.
Nana had told me you deciphered
notes by ear. After years of lessons
you recited the classics back to teachers
with those thin, striving fingers,
then tucked away your certificates,
texts and sheet music, graduating
with honours. Yet everyday afterwards
a new, unlearned melody moved you,
the way the sun touches the bay,
rhythmic pulse of the years beat to the fall
of your steps, and you went back
to the black and ivory keys to teach yourself
what could not be taught, like a boy
conceiving love after being warned about it.
Slowly and perfectly it fell from you,
not notes but movement, the unbroken
throb of your forty years of playing.
I hear what you profess, back straight,
those rough aged hands, face exalted,
and the music inspiring, exhaling,
the ceaseless song of graduation.

Last Rites

There was no blood. When I ran
to my grandmother's bedroom
where she was dying in her bed
I had expected a sign of murder,
but her heart could not ignite the blood,
the valves like oars had tired.
Her mouth and eyes were opening
and closing like gills. I sat her up
in the bed and leaned her against
my shoulder, heavy like a wet towel.
Almost asleep under the last heat
of her body, she could not hear
all the hearts in the house beating
like wings. When her eyes jerked open
she cried out, *Am I going to die?*
She was three-quarters deaf, and I loved
that I was one-quarter of this woman,
my father had swum in her and I floated
in some chamber of her pure body, utterly alive.
I loved that there was still a portion
of my grandmother vital and listening.
I held her ear to my mouth and spoke
to the fraction of her that could decipher.
I said, You are never leaving. I felt
I spoke to her outside the realm of sound,
as if we were making a communion
in the woods and saw, in a clearing,
branches parting and light breaking
in the dark, fragile as the drops of sweat
on her chest as I leant down to kiss her heart.
I would have believed she could hear me,
but when the priest walked in he took
her hand as it went limp, a fallen leaf,
and she did not hear the prayers. You're there
with your crook and staff, Grandmother,
with these you've given me courage.
And to the ears of some deaf Angel
I whisper, *Amen*, my love.

Say Goodbye

My grandmother's death was everywhere;
it was the absence of traffic, the lone walker
stepping along the path of his torch.
I felt pregnant with the moment
it took for her last breath to grasp us,
uttering something from a great distance,
forcing us to hear. My brother and I
walked outside, around the hospital,
like birds who'd flown away at the sound
of thunder. We walked, hand in hand,
across the car park, the life-blood
ebbing away from our grandmother.
We could have been walking away from death,
stepping across the blocks of concrete
like continents splitting between
our grandmother and ourselves.

And suddenly we were standing
in front of the ward where I had tried
to die. My eyes closed with shock,
as if I'd arrived there like a meteor before
it hit the earth, pulling with it roots
from old soil.
          I wanted to break a window
of that casket, smash the artery full of poison.
I fell heavily against the cold pillars
and howled, as if grief itself
would haul down that grey house.
But my brother took my hand, led me back
for the last time to our grandmother's body.
Like a cat with her immutable lives,
I stood up. I felt it was time
to leave that coffin.

The Past

I look on it now as I do the people
whose names I can never remember.
The people I knew in that past
are skeletons. They spill like milk
from room to room in some unnameable house.
Even now I cannot remember them well.
I know the empty townlands they contrived,
the epitaphs on the headstones.
But memories have a strange lexicon,
like the old English plays I studied
at school but never understood,
except for the comma, the period,
the exclamation, the aftertaste of emotion.

Sometimes I go back to that unlit house
where bones and ribs gather to sit
and stare. Their hearts have escaped
from those mouldy prisons. I see,
through darkness soggy with calcium,
the bare room, coffee tables wall-to-wall,
the drunken labyrinth between them,
heavy doors that blow open like sudden breath.
But there is no breath in this ancestry,
we do not mention life here, only smile
maniacally, leaving doors hanging,
the bath running, the cupboards
empty, perishing in the memory
of warm blood. And the sickness,
whatever its poison, was a lover.

This Time

She sat on the ground outside the pub,
her head slipping from the drunken
grip of her hands. I held her hair
back while she heaved the night's
sorrows, moaning that this was
the worst night ever, that life was hell.

I could see her hands going limp,
how the mind could not support the body,
and how the body punishes the mind,
an endless globe. I could not take my eyes
off her, a child slowly disappearing
into a pool of beer and vomit on the ground.

When I got home I washed away
my garish eyeliner, the blood-red
lipstick, and suddenly I saw myself
in the mirror, unmasked, eyes wide
without the hood of black pencil.
I saw a face, pale as it was
when I was a child.

I was looking at this girl as if
we were two separate beings clinging
to the sink. She seemed to float towards me
as the mirror vanished. Watching her
move towards me, I saw her frailty,
how easily she could fall when running,
her arms outstretched, eyes fiercely innocent.
Child, I will not harm you again.

The Therapist

Without touch he seems to hold on
with a gentle grip, folding around me,
leaving me with bruises I can never find.

This love was unmoving, but lately I have
seen it stir, its bruise-purple colour expanding
towards my body, the way the ocean exhales
when you reach the edge of a cliff.

I have always felt him holding onto me –
not my body but my soul, that sweet, indigo throat
being nourished. In his room this love enters me
and I feel as if it's my own spirit enfolding me,

the way a bird can wrap its wings around itself.
When I see my spirit opening unto me
I think of the nights I would crawl
into bed with my parents, a storm
galloping madly around us.

They pressed against my body as if
I were the septum against
which the heart throbs, and I thought
I was being conceived again between

the gold mist of flesh. And now,
I don't want those arms to be my parents.
I don't want a child's breakable skin
or the hands that cannot grip another's.

I want the world new and strange –
to be placed into the arms
of another, my eyes opening
in the confidence of love,

my spirit waking to it.

Graduating

Before I climb into the taxi I turn
to look one more time at my mother.
She looks much smaller, younger as
she leans in the doorway of our house,
one hand on her stomach, the other
waving me gently away. I had never
really thought much about *her*,
a soul that trembled above me, beside me,
ahead of me. Last night she helped me
pack away my clothes, like folding vestments
at the end of a Mass. I looked at her
whole body, trying to see life without her,
her tapered fingers, her father's lips,
the old topography of her belly where
I once lay my entire small body,
egg-curled in her palms. Or the nights
I went to her as she wept, climbing
over her into the bed, without a word,
and drew her into my chest. I stroked
her hair, soothing the nape of her neck,
her cheek upon my heart.
She had taught me this, this love
of the womb, and I recited it to her,
reading every inch of my life like braille.
I think of you, Mother, across a road,
leaning against a door frame, standing
in a meadow, your head tilted towards
the sun, throwing up your arms
and taking me into you, kissing my cheeks,
like blood pulsing to the heart, root to thorn
to flower. In the car I glimpse her
in the mirror, still waving, her fingers drawing
a fragile arc as if she were guiding me back.
I sit quietly, moving out to the edge
of the world – the edge I saw when I believed
the world to be flat, before my mother
taught me it was round.

Waiting for My Clothes

The day the doctors and nurses are having
their weekly patient interviews, I sit waiting
my turn outside the office, my back to the wall,
legs curled up under my chin, playing

with the hem of my white hospital gown.
They have taken everything they thought
should be taken – my clothes, my books,
my music, as if being stripped of these

were part of the cure, like removing the sheath
from a blade that has slaughtered.
They said, Wait a few days, and if you're good
you can have your things back. They'd taken

my journal, my word made flesh, and I think
of those doctors knowing me naked,
holding me by my spine, two fingers
under my neck, the way you would hold a baby,

taking my soul from between my ribs
and leafing through the pages of my thoughts,
as if they were reading my palms,
and my name beneath them like a confession,

owning this girl, claiming this world
of blackness and lightness and death
and birth. It lies in their hands like a life-line,
and I feel myself fall open or apart.

They hear my voice as they read
and think, Who is this girl that is speaking?
I know the end, she tells them.
It is the last line, both source and closing.

It is what oceans sing to, how the sun moves,
a place for the map-maker to begin.
Behind the door, nothing is said.
Like dreams, my clothes come out of their boxes.